HOW TO IMPROVE AT GYMNASTICS

**All the information you need to know
to get on top of your game!**

More than just instructional guides, the **HOW TO IMPROVE AT...** series gives you everything you need to achieve your goals — tips on technique, step-by-step demonstrations, nutritional advice, and the secrets of successful pro athletes. Excellent visual instructions and expert advice combine to act as your own personal trainer. These books aim to give you the know-how and confidence to improve your performance.

Studies have shown that an active approach to life makes you feel happier and less stressed. The easiest way to start is by taking up a new sport or improving your skills in an existing one. You simply have to choose an activity that enthuses you.

HOW TO IMPROVE AT GYMNASTICS does not promise instant success. It simply gives you the tools to become the best at whatever you choose to do.

Every care has been taken to ensure that these instructions are safe to follow, but in the event of injury Crabtree Publishing shall not be liable for any injuries or damages.

Heather Brown is a freelance writer and is the founder of the global publication, Backflip Gymnastics Magazine. She holds a Masters degree in Journalism and a Bsc Hons degree in Sport, Exercise & Leisure

*ticktock Media Ltd
would like to thank the following:
Alpha Factor: for the supply of clothing;
Woking Gymnastics Club:
Sarah Calvert (advisor),
Natalie Reeve (coach),
Simon Elliott (coach),
Connor, Megan, Katie & Samuel;
Pegasus Gymnastics Club:
Ionut Trandaburu (coach) & Courtney.*

Crabtree Publishing Company
www.crabtreebooks.com

Author: Heather Brown
Editors: Reagan Miller, Annabel Savery
Proofreader: Crystal Sikkens
Project coordinator: Robert Walker
Prepress technician: Margaret Amy Salter
Production coordinator: Margaret Amy Salter

Planning and production by Discovery Books Ltd.

Designer: Graham Rich
Managing Editor: Rachel Tisdale
Photographer: Chris Fairclough

Photo credits:

Getty Images: AFP: p. 46 (inset); Allsport UK:
    p. 46 (main); Frank Fife: p. 47 (left); Stu Forster:
    p. 47 (right); Mark Nolan: p. 43; Friedman Vogel: p. 42

Library and Archives Canada Cataloguing in Publication

Brown, Heather E
    How to improve at gymnastics / Heather E. Brown.

(How to improve at--)
Includes index.
ISBN 978-0-7787-3573-1 (bound).--ISBN 978-0-7787-3595-3 (pbk.)

    1. Gymnastics--Juvenile literature.
I. Title. II. Series: How to improve at--

GV461.3.B44 2009   j796.44   C2008-907842-X

Library of Congress Cataloging-in-Publication Data

Brown, Heather E.
    How to improve at gymnastics / Heather E. Brown.
        p. cm. -- (How to improve at--)
    Includes index.
    ISBN 978-0-7787-3595-3 (pbk. : alk. paper) -- ISBN 978-0-7787-3573-1
(reinforced library binding : alk. paper)
    1. Gymnastics--Juvenile literature. I. Title. II. Series.

GV461.B36 2009
796.44--dc22

                                                    2008052118

Crabtree Publishing Company
www.crabtreebooks.com   1-800-387-7650

**Published in Canada
Crabtree Publishing**
616 Welland Ave.
St. Catharines, Ontario
L2M 5V6

**Published in the United States
Crabtree Publishing**
PMB16A
350 Fifth Ave., Suite 3308
New York, NY 10118

CONTENTS

INTRODUCTION

G ymnastics is a fun and dynamic sport for everyone. It's a great way to stay fit and healthy and to learn new skills. You can also make good friends at your club and you will have the opportunity to travel and perform in competitions together.

HISTORY OF GYMNASTICS

Gymnastics is one of the oldest Olympic sports. It was included in the first modern Olympic Games, held in Athens in 1896. On that occasion, 285 athletes—all of them men—competed in the Games. Women gymnasts first competed in the Olympics at the 1928 Games, held in Amsterdam. The high levels of artistry and technical skill in gymnastics make it a popular spectator sport around the world.

GUIDE TO ARROWS

Throughout the book we have used red arrows like this ➡ to indicate the action and direction of the body.

EQUIPMENT

In artistic gymnastics, women compete in four events: vault, asymmetric bars, beam, and floor. Men compete in six events: floor, vault, pommel horse, rings, parallel bars, and high bar.

VAULT

Gymnasts run down a runway that is padded or carpeted and hurdle onto the springboard. They then spring onto the vaulting table with their hands and push off into the air before landing on a landing mat on the other side. While in the air, gymnasts might perform moves, such as twists and somersaults, before landing (see pages 10–13).

Vaulting table

Springboard

All the pieces of apparatus are arranged in the gym so that gymnasts can use them safely.

FLOOR

The floor area is made of wooden panels mounted on springs (known as a spring floor) and covered in carpet. The spring floor enables gymnasts to perform tumbling sequences. Floor routines feature acrobatics, leaps, jumps, turns, and dance (see pages 14-17). The edge of the floor area is marked with a line and you lose points if you step outside this area.

PARALLEL BARS

Consisting of rails made of fiberglass and wood, the parallel bars are set at the same height and are the same length. Male gymnasts perform swinging movements which allow them to rotate above and below the bars (see pages 18–21).

RINGS

The rings hang nine feet (2.75 m) above the floor from cables that are attached to the ceiling. The rings are 19.7 inches (50 cm) apart and gymnasts must perform a routine involving swinging and strength skills (see pages 22–25).

ASYMMETRIC BARS

Also known as the "uneven bars," the asymmetric bars consist of two bars set at different heights. A springboard can be used to mount the apparatus. In competition, a routine on the asymmetric bars must be continuous, without any stops or extra swings (see pages 26–29).

Springboard

When practicing, gymnasts use thick safety mats to land on. These are soft and will break their fall.

POMMEL HORSE

The pommel horse has two handles (or pommels) attached to it and two legs that are secured to the floor. Gymnasts perform a routine of skills including scissors and circles using the whole length of the horse (see pages 30-33).

BALANCE BEAM

Gymnasts tumble and dance along a balance beam that stands four feet (1.2 m) above the floor. The beam is four inches (10 cm) wide. Gymnasts must practice balance and control when performing on the beam (see pages 34–37).

Selection of beams for different levels of gymnasts.

HIGH BAR

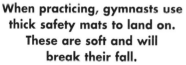

The high bar is a single bar standing 9.2 feet (2.8 m) high. The bar is made of polished steel. Gymnasts perform release skills high above the bar, and dismount with multiple somersaults or twists (see pages 38–41).

WHAT TO WEAR & TRAINING

In competition, women gymnasts wear leotards. These can be long sleeved or short sleeved. Male gymnasts generally wear a singlet and shorts, but for the pommel horse, parallel bars, rings, and high bar they wear long gymnastics pants instead of shorts. They also wear socks when performing on these events. The long pants allow the judges to see a gymnast's body line when he performs his routines.

Leotards

Shorts

Long gymnastics pants

FOOTWEAR

Many gymnasts prefer to work barefoot, however special footwear is permitted in competition for both men and women gymnasts. Gymnastics slippers should be in good condition, have non-slip soles, and fit well. Gymnasts should never wear jewelry, in training or in competition, as it could cause an injury. Long hair should be tied back to avoid distraction.

GRIPS

When performing on the asymmetric bars many gymnasts wear handguards or grips. These protect the hands from injuries, such as blisters. Traditional grips are made from a variety of materials, such as leather or suede.

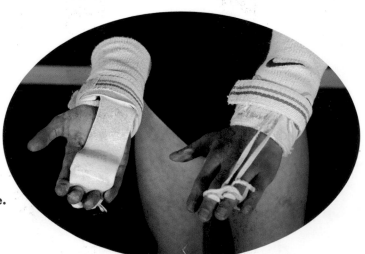

Leotards

Long gymnastics pants

TRAINING

Elite gymnasts preparing for World Championships and the Olympic Games can train for as many as 40 hours per week. It takes hard work, commitment, a love of the sport, and natural talent to become a world gymnastics champion. Hours of practice are needed to reach the top in gymnastics, and as elite gymnasts progress, so too does the time they need to invest in training.

PARENTAL SUPPORT

This tough training program requires support from parents and from schools, as gymnasts need flexible timetables to allow them to train during the day and to travel to competitions.

PHYSICAL PREPARATION

To advance in gymnastics, you must prepare your body physically by doing strength and flexibility exercises. Your coach should prepare a strength-training program for you that suits your age and physical development and addresses your areas of weakness.

Flexibility is very important too. Flexibility is the range of movement in a joint. It allows you to perform skills correctly and protects you from injuries.

CHALK

Using magnesium carbonate or chalk will help you keep your grip and prevent you from slipping when performing on bar events. Chalk absorbs perspiration and allows you to keep contact with the bars. It helps to prevent blisters, as it reduces friction between the bars and your hands.

WARMING UP & STRETCHING

*Y*ou must *warm up* before you begin any form of physical activity. Warming up prepares your body for exercise as it increases the blood flow to your muscles and provides them with added oxygen. The warm-up will also mentally prepare you for your training session ahead and reduce the chance of injury. Once you have warmed up by running or jogging around your gym, you should do some stretching exercises.

QUADRICEPS STRETCH

Lift one foot behind you and hold it in your hand. Keep your knees close together. Your standing foot should be flat. Hold the position for 10 seconds and repeat with the other leg. You will feel the stretch down the front of your thigh.

SHOULDER STRETCH

Hold one arm straight out in front of you. Move it across your body and apply pressure with the inside of your elbow of the other arm. Hold the stretch for 10 seconds and repeat with the other arm.

BRIDGE

Start lying on your back with your knees bent and your hands on the floor by the side of your head. Push through your shoulders to extend your back into an arch shape. To exit out of the bridge gently bend your knees and your elbows and lower your body to the ground. This is a good exercise to warm up your back.

Keep your legs and arms as straight as possible.

ROCKING

Sit with your knees bent, hug them and place your hands on both shins. Lift your feet and point your toes. Gently rock forward and backward. You should do this after you have done a bridge, as it helps relax your back muscles.

TOP TIP
*It is important to stretch your muscles gently.
If you force your stretching, you may injure yourself.*

THE SPLITS

Left leg splits

By practicing the splits, you will increase the flexibility in your hips and hamstrings. There are three positions in which the splits can be performed: with the right leg in front, the left leg in front, and the straddle, or middle, splits.

STRADDLE STRETCH

The straddle position is where your legs are spread wide in front of you. Sit up straight in the straddle position. Your legs should be straight and toes pointed. Reach your arms out to the sides.

Toes pointed

FORWARD STRADDLE STRETCH

Sit in the straddle position with your knees facing toward the ceiling and your toes pointed. Try to lie your chest flat on the floor in front of you.

THE SWIM THROUGH

This technique will stretch your inner thigh muscles, try and relax into the stretch and hold for 10 seconds.

STEP 1

Sit in the straddle position. Stretch forward and lie your chest flat on the floor in front of you. Stretch your legs back into the middle splits position.

Middle splits position

STEP 2

Bring your legs together and finish lying on your stomach in a straight position.

Finish position for the swim through

TOP TIP
Wear your tracksuit during warm-up sessions to prevent your body temperature from dropping.

VAULT

Vaulting is fast and dynamic. Gymnasts run at high speed along a runway, jump onto the springboard, reach for the vaulting table, and propel themselves high into the air, landing safely on the other side of the apparatus.

THE HURDLE STEP

To practice your hurdle step technique, take off from the springboard and do a straight jump onto a safety mat. Repeat this exercise until you gain confidence, then move on to the vault runway.

Lean forward into the run.

STEP 1

Run up to the springboard with speed and determination. Lean forward into the run with your head looking straight toward the vault. When you reach the springboard, start to push off from the ground with your front foot.

Push off with your front foot.

STEP 2

As you push off from your front foot, lift your back foot and swing both legs forward with your knees slightly bent to land near the end of the springboard.

Take your arms behind your body.

STEP 3

Bend your knees slightly when you land on the springboard, and take your arms behind your body. This will lower your chest and assist with the forward drive on to the vault. Push off from the springboard with both feet.

Land on the springboard with both feet.

STEP 4

*Land on the safety mat in the **demi-plié** position. Your back should be straight and your hips, knees, and ankles should be bent.*

Keep your arms straight.

Keep your knees bent.

Practice doing a handstand against a wall.

THE HANDSTAND

The handstand is a key skill for the vault. Practice doing a handstand on the floor and against a wall.

*When you are in your handstand position, shrug your shoulders up and down, this is a good way to learn the technique of "**blocking**." Blocking is when you keep your arms fully extended and straight and push through your shoulders.*

TOP TIP

Improve your speed by practicing timed sprints up the vault runway.

THE HANDSPRING VAULT

The handspring is a key skill in vaulting. This is an important move for any young gymnast to master. Advanced progressions include somersaults and twisting. The aim is to have a tight body throughout the handstand phase and achieve a good flight off the vault. The handspring vault is broken down into five stages.

THE HANDSPRING VAULT

STEP 1
TAKE OFF
Have a strong, fast run up. Your feet should make contact with the springboard in front of your body. Your knees should be slightly bent and your feet should be parallel.

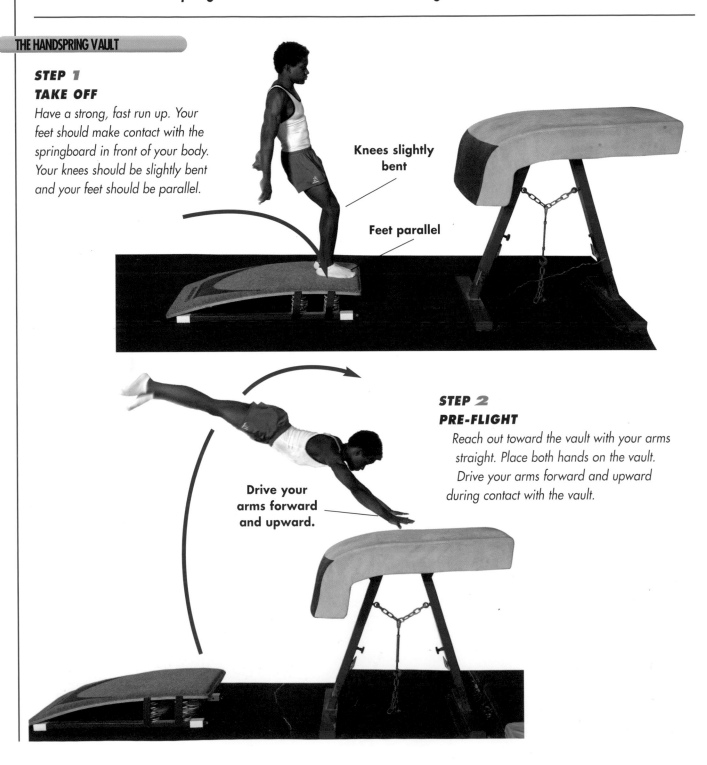

Knees slightly bent

Feet parallel

STEP 2
PRE-FLIGHT
Reach out toward the vault with your arms straight. Place both hands on the vault. Drive your arms forward and upward during contact with the vault.

Drive your arms forward and upward.

STEP 3
THE THRUST FROM THE HANDS

Before your body reaches a vertical position, block, or rebound, off the vault by pushing your arms against the vault. This thrust through your arms must be powerful and rapid so you gain height and distance off the vaulting table.

Keep your body straight.

STEP 4
POST FLIGHT

Make sure your body is tight and straight in the air.

Keep your body straight.

Use your arms and hands to push off from the vault.

Back straight

Hips, knees, and ankles bent

STEP 5
LANDING

Land safely in a demi-plié position. Your back should be straight and your hips, knees, and ankles should be bent.

TOP TIP
The time spent on the springboard should be quick so that you don't lose any speed or power.

FLOOR

Floor routines can be the most spectacular events in gymnatics. On the floor gymnasts can demonstrate impressive acrobatic movements. As women's floor routines are set to music they are particularly popular with audiences and they allow gymnasts to express their personality through dance and musical style.

CHOREOGRAPHY

Choreographers **work with top-class gymnasts to create their floor routines.** Choreographers help gymnasts create expressive dance movements in between tumbling passes. Gymnasts and choreographers work together to choose music that suits the athlete's personality.

BALLET

Ballet training from an early age teaches good posture, coordination, and spacial awareness. It also develops **poise** and grace as it improves strength and flexibility. Gymnasts often stand at a **ballet bar** in front of a mirror. This helps them to correct and improve their technique.

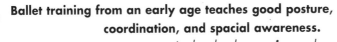

Gymnast at a bar

Demi-plié

Gymnast performing expressive dance

THE HANDSTAND

The handstand is a fundamental move in gymnastics and it is essential to master it in order to move on to more challenging skills. It is performed on all pieces of apparatus. Have a fun competition with your teammates and see who can stay up in a handstand for the longest amount of time. The more you practice, the more strength you will build up in your arms and shoulders and the easier it will become to hold it for longer.

STEP 1
Stand up tall with your body fully stretched and your arms straight above your head.

STEP 2
Raise your lead leg and step into a deep lunge.

Raise lead leg

STEP 3
Lean over and move your chest down toward the thigh of your lead leg. The angle between your arms and your chest should remain fully open.

Lunge forward

STEP 4
Place your hands on the floor in front of your lead foot.

STEP 5
Kick into the handstand, this should be a controlled swinging movement of the leg. Your upper body should be in line with your hands. Hold your body tight in a **hollow** *position, with your feet pointed and legs together.*

Maintain your balance through your hands and control at your shoulders.

TOP TIP
Practice holding your tight body position in a handstand against a wall.

CARTWHEELS & BACK HANDSPRINGS

Cartwheels are one of the most basic skills in gymnastics. Practicing and perfecting the cartwheel will develop your upper body and leg strength. By practicing the splits, you will be able to achieve a wider straddle in the cartwheel. Always keep your arms and legs straight.

CARTWHEELS

When you have perfected your cartwheel, you can learn more advanced skills, such as a one-handed cartwheel, and a round off, which is when you join your two feet together at the end of a cartwheel.

STEP 1
Lift your lead leg to get momentum.

Lift lead leg.

STEP 2
Step forward with a lunge.

Twist your upper body sideways as your chest lowers to the floor.

Put your hands down.

Swing back leg up.

Swing your back leg up, thrust from your lead leg, and put your hands down.

Straddle position.

STEP 3
In the air your legs will pass through the straddle position.

STEP 4
Bring your leading leg downward and place close to your hand.

Bring your leg down close to your hand.

Lift your body up by pushing through your hands.

STEP 5
Place your second leg in line with your first leg.

TOP TIP
Practice doing cartwheels one after another in a row and see if you can stay in a straight line.

BACK HANDSPRING

STEP 1

Stand tall with your arms straight up by your ears.

The back handspring is one of the most popular moves for an aspiring gymnast to learn as it allows you to travel backward with speed. Advanced gymnasts who perform tumbling passes use the back handspring as an accelerator, as it makes it possible to go faster backward and rebound into harder moves, such as back saltos and twists.

STEP 2

Bend your knees so that you are in a slight sitting position. Lean backward and keep your heels down. Your knees must remain in line with your toes.

Knees in line with toes

STEP 4

Remember to keep your legs together and straight.

STEP 3

Rotate backward with a strong arm swing.

Keep your arms straight.

STEP 5

Spring up quickly from your hands to your feet. As you push through your shoulders, keep your arms straight and your legs will come straight over your head.

STEP 6

Land with your arms up by your ears. Bend your knees to give you a soft landing.

Push through with your hands and shoulders.

TOP TIP
Always remember that your hands should be parallel in the back handspring.

PARALLEL BARS

You need good upper body strength to perform on the parallel bars. You can adjust the width of the parallel bars to suit your height. Usually the width between the bars is set at the same distance as the length between your elbow and the tips of your fingers. A competition routine on the parallel bars consists of swings, flight movements, and strength elements. It ends with a dismount off the end or the side of the parallel bars.

STRENGTH HOLDS

To build up the upper body strength required for this event, you must work on strength holds. *These are static skills which you should aim to hold for three seconds, without any movement or swinging.*

TUCKED HOLD

Tucked hold

Start with your body hanging down in a straight position. *Your arms and shoulders should be locked on the bars to keep you in position. Keep your arms straight. Bend your knees and bring them both gently up to your chest.*

Keep your arms straight.

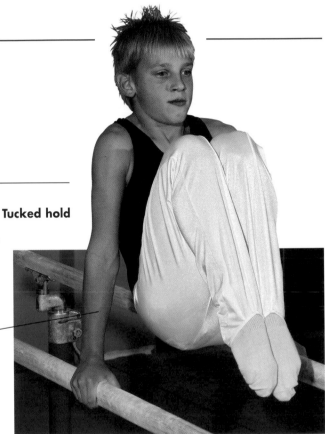

LEG LIFTS ON A BOX TOP

Parallettes

To practice for the lever position on the parallel bars, start on the parallettes by doing sets of leg lifts on a box top.

Parallettes are smaller and lower than parallel bars. Place the box top across them and rest your legs on it. Keep your arms locked to support your weight.

Try going into the lever position holding one leg at a time, leave one leg on top of the box and when you feel ready, raise it up to join the other one to form the lever position.

Box top

THE LEVER POSITION

Once you feel confident and you have built up your strength, you can try holding the lever position without the aid of the box top.

Like many moves in gymnastics, you can perform them on other pieces of apparatus, such as the floor or on the rings.

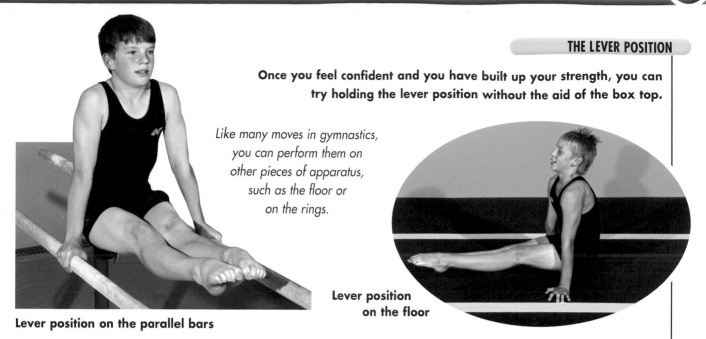

Lever position on the parallel bars

Lever position on the floor

RUSSIAN LEVER

A lot of body conditioning **is required in order to hold a Russian lever.**

Once you are in a piked position (with your legs straight and your body bent at the hips), try to bring your legs up toward your face, keeping them straight and controlled. The Russian lever takes many gymnasts a long time to master. To make it easier, try doing the tucked hold, which will mean your legs are bent, and then try and straighten them out and upward.

Russian lever on the parallel bars

STRADDLE LEVER

Another good strength hold is the straddle lever.
First you need to sit on the floor in straddle position. Keep your stomach muscles tight and toes pointed, lift yourself up off the ground. To balance, spread your fingers and keep them flat on the floor. Make sure your legs stay straight. When you feel confident, then you can try to perform this lever on the parallel bars with the help of your coach.

Straddle lever on the floor

THE BASKET SWING

A basket swing is a swing where your shoulders and body are piked and your center of gravity lies between your shoulders. This is a difficult move because you must learn how to create the swing. By practicing this on a rail, it is easier to understand the movement that you need to create on two bars. The amount that you swing is also very short, so it's difficult to gain momentum.

THE BASKET SWING

STEP 1

To get into the position for the basket swing you must go into the inverted pike position. This is where you are hanging upside down with your legs straight and close to your chest.

Hold on to the bars, with your arms straight and your chest facing the ceiling. Kick both legs up so your knees are in front of your face.

Keep your arms and legs straight and start the swing from your shoulders.

Your hands should be on the inside of the bars.

Body in inverted pike position

STEP 2

Keep your head tucked in as you use your shoulders to bring your body forward.

Keep your head tucked in.

STEP 3
Lift your shoulders and hips upward and forward. Try not to bend. Remember this is a swinging movement, so it is through your shoulders that you will gain the momentum that you need.

Lift shoulders

Lift hips

STEP 4
Keep a tight body position throughout the move. In order to get more swing, pike more at the beginning of the swing as you swing downward and then open out on the upward phase.

TOP TIP
Practice sitting on the floor in a piked position and lean over with a straight back to lie your chest flat on to your knees. Keep your knees and arms straight. This will increase the flexibility in your hamstrings.

RINGS: BASIC SWING

*T*he key to a good swinging technique is a well-conditioned body and the ability to maintain a tight body shape throughout the movement. The swing is a key element on the rings, so you should spend a long time practicing it.

THE BASIC SWING

STEP 1
Your body should be tight and in a slightly arched shape, and your arms must be straight at all times.

Arms straight

Arch shape

STEP 2
Your hips should relax when your body approaches the hang position (when your body is hanging straight), midway through the swing.

Your body should be straight at the hips in the downswing.

STEP 3
Your feet lead to allow aggressive drive of the legs through the bottom of the swing. In the upswing your feet should lead the swing. Your body should form a deep hollow at the hips.

Hollow at the hips

Feet lead the swing

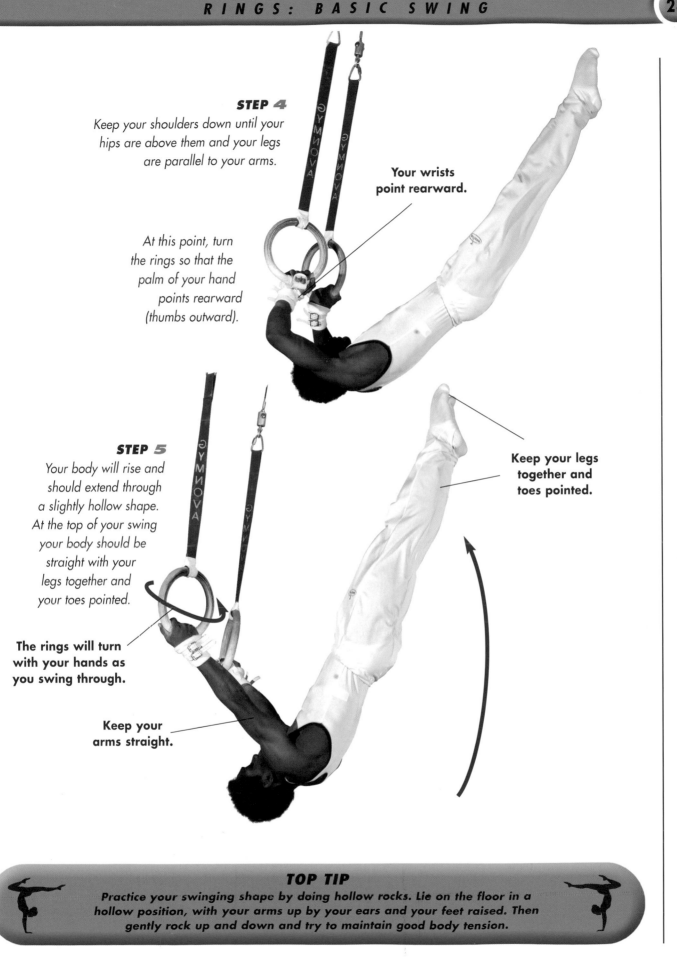

STEP 4

Keep your shoulders down until your hips are above them and your legs are parallel to your arms.

Your wrists point rearward.

At this point, turn the rings so that the palm of your hand points rearward (thumbs outward).

Keep your legs together and toes pointed.

STEP 5

Your body will rise and should extend through a slightly hollow shape. At the top of your swing your body should be straight with your legs together and your toes pointed.

The rings will turn with your hands as you swing through.

Keep your arms straight.

TOP TIP

Practice your swinging shape by doing hollow rocks. Lie on the floor in a hollow position, with your arms up by your ears and your feet raised. Then gently rock up and down and try to maintain good body tension.

RINGS

Swinging and strength holds are the main elements of
a rings routine. You need good technique in swinging
momentum and the ability to hold yourself in a strength hold.
This requires tremendous body conditioning.

Tucked hold

STATIC STRENGTH HOLDS

**Like on the parallel bars, static strength holds are very important
and require practice in order to control and balance the movements.**
*You can lower the rings closer to the floor, which will make practicing your
strength holds easier.*

TUCKED HOLD

Practice the tucked hold on the rings.
A **tuck** *position is when you have your knees bent and pulled up
to your chest. Remember to keep your toes pointed and head
looking up, and don't be tempted to swing!*

HALF LEVER HOLD ON A BOX TOP

**Once you have mastered holding the
tuck position you can attempt the
half lever hold.**
*This takes a lot of strength to hold and
control. To practice, use a box top, and
lift one leg up at a time. This is useful if
you find it too difficult to lift both legs
up together.*

THE HALF LEVER POSITION

**Once you feel
confident, raise the
rings up to the
correct height and
practice the lever
hold in the air.**
*You might need your
coach to help lift you
up to the rings.*

Toes pointed
toward the
ceiling

Legs
straight

To perform a series of swings and holds, such as straddle and pike, and then to eventually push up to a handstand on the rings, requires great strength and balance. These drills will improve your balance and control.

INVERTED HANG

The inverted hang will help to develop your balance.
To get into the move kick over into a piked hold—which means your legs will be straight and close to your body. Then push your legs up as high up as you can into a straight body position.

GERMAN OR BACK HANG

To get into the German or back hang position, hold on to the rings with straight arms and bring your legs up into a tucked position.
Then invert yourself, which means hanging upside down. Bring your feet through your hands and over your head and start to straighten them as much as you can and extend through your shoulders.

German
or back
hang

PIKED INVERTED HANG

Hang upside down, bring your legs straight down together toward your face.
The more flexible your hamstrings are, the easier it will be to hang in a pike position.

Piked
inverted
hang

TOP TIP
*Practice holding the half lever by using the support of a box top.
Using this as a platform will help you to balance and to build up strength
in your abdominal area.*

ASYMMETRIC BARS

The most important skill on the asymmetric bars is the ability to swing. You need a natural fluid swing with good rhythm to perform the high-level release moves which are required in elite gymnastics. In competition, your bar routine must be continuous with no stops. The routine must include skills on the low bar and the high bar, release elements, and a dismount.

TYPES OF GRASP

The most common hand grasps used in gymnastics on the bars are the undergrip and the overgrip.

UNDERGRIP

Your hands grip the bar with your palms facing toward you.

OVERGRIP

Your hands grip the bar with your palms facing away from you.

BODY CONDITIONING EXERCISES ON THE BARS

Your gymnastics training should include some body conditioning to improve your strength.
Using the bars is an important part of body conditioning, as it helps to improve your upper body strength. You should perform all of these exercises slowly and with control. Do not swing into the movements, as this means you are not using all of your body strength.

CHIN-UPS

Chin-ups will greatly improve your upper body strength.
At first, you may not be able to pull yourself right up to the bar. Your coach can help you with this by holding on to your legs and helping to lift your body weight up so your chin reaches the bar.

Keep your arms straight before you pull up, so you are hanging with a straight body. Bend at the elbows and use your upper arm muscles to pull your chin up to the bar.

Do not swing in to the chin-up as you won't be using the right muscles.

LEG LIFTS

Hang on the bar with your arms and legs extended. Raise your legs upward toward the bar, so your toes touch it.
Your legs should be straight and toes pointed throughout. This exercise will strengthen your stomach muscles, which are called your abdominals.

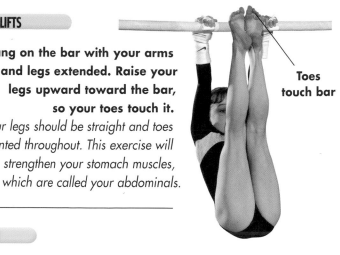

Toes touch bar

BODY POSITIONS

In order to have a good swinging technique on the bars, you must learn the correct body positions that you should be achieving in a swing.
There are two key parts of the swing which you should learn. These are the arch and the hollow body positions.

ARCH

Lie on your stomach and put your arms above your head.
Keep your arms and your legs straight and lift them up off the floor as high as you can.

HOLLOW HOLD

Lie on your back and put your arms above your head.
Keep your arms and your legs straight and, as in the arch movement, lift them as high as you can. The higher you go, the more your legs will want to separate, but it is important to keep them together and only go as far as you can in the hollow body position.

PRACTICING BODY POSITIONS

Just like on the floor, you can practice holding the same arch and hollow positions while hanging on the bar. When moving between the arch and hollow positions, you will pass through a straight hanging position.

Hanging in hollow   **Straight position**   **Hanging in arch**

TOP TIP
You can purchase a single bar that will fit onto your door frame at home, so you can practice your conditioning exercises, such as chin-ups and leg lifts.

THE GLIDE KIP

*T*he glide kip is a very important linking skill on the bars. It is the first move used by many gymnasts to begin their asymmetric bars routine. As a linking move, it allows the gymnast to build up momentum to perform additional, more difficult skills, such as casting up to a handstand.

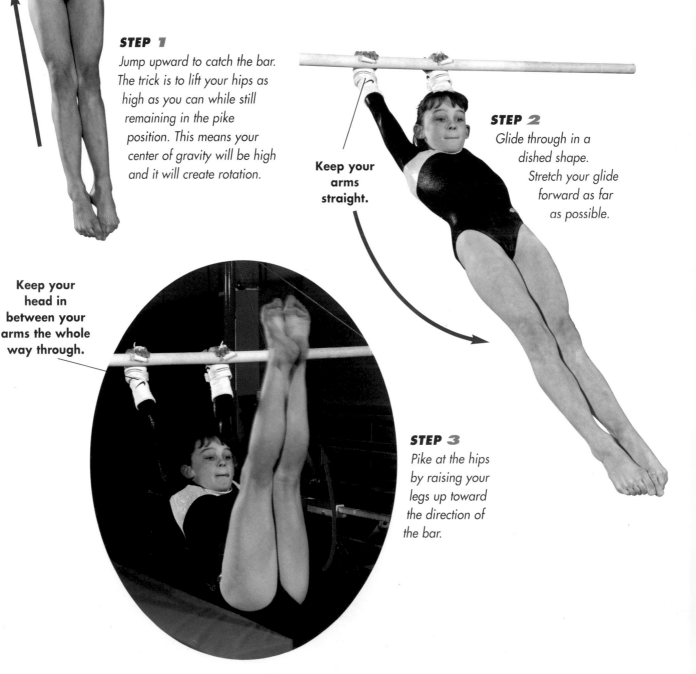

STEP 1

Jump upward to catch the bar. The trick is to lift your hips as high as you can while still remaining in the pike position. This means your center of gravity will be high and it will create rotation.

Keep your arms straight.

STEP 2

Glide through in a dished shape. Stretch your glide forward as far as possible.

Keep your head in between your arms the whole way through.

STEP 3

Pike at the hips by raising your legs up toward the direction of the bar.

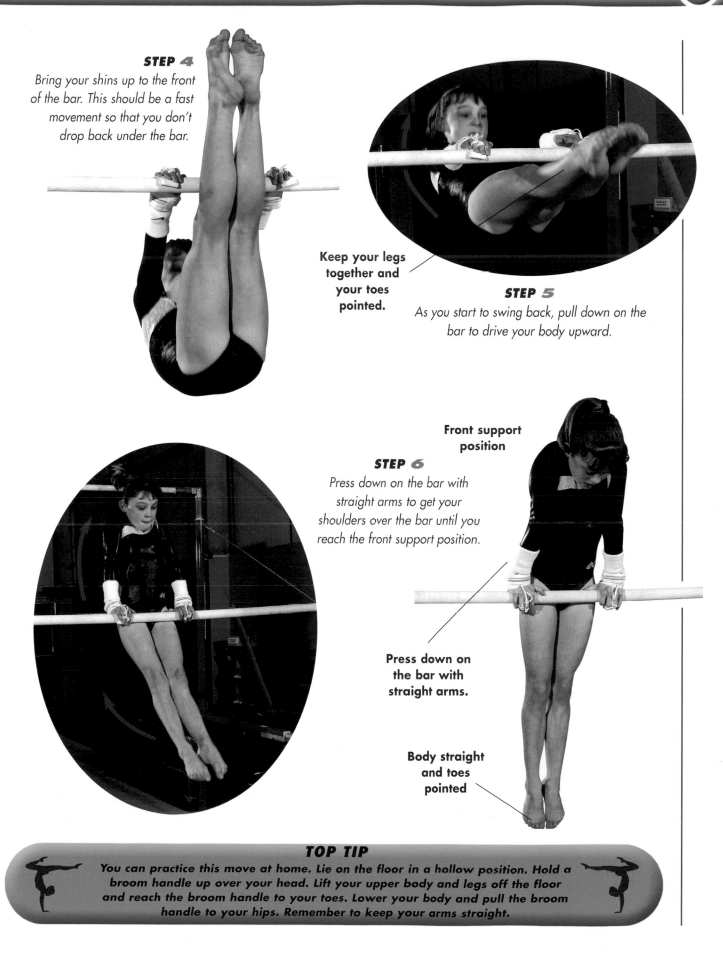

STEP 4

Bring your shins up to the front of the bar. This should be a fast movement so that you don't drop back under the bar.

Keep your legs together and your toes pointed.

STEP 5

As you start to swing back, pull down on the bar to drive your body upward.

Front support position

STEP 6

Press down on the bar with straight arms to get your shoulders over the bar until you reach the front support position.

Press down on the bar with straight arms.

Body straight and toes pointed

TOP TIP

You can practice this move at home. Lie on the floor in a hollow position. Hold a broom handle up over your head. Lift your upper body and legs off the floor and reach the broom handle to your toes. Lower your body and pull the broom handle to your hips. Remember to keep your arms straight.

POMMEL HORSE

A typical pommel horse routine involves single and double leg work, known as scissors and circles. Double leg work in the form of circles makes up most of a routine at the elite level. This involves the gymnast swinging both legs around the pommels in a circular motion.

LEVELS OF DIFFICULTY

This piece of apparatus is technically very difficult as the gymnast's hands are the only part of his body that are in contact.

Although it requires a lot of strength, technique is probably even more important. To increase the difficulty, a gymnast will add circling and turning movements. Flairs are also a popular skill, which is when the gymnast straddles his legs wide and can circle the pommels. In a competition routine, you must include traveling movements and use all parts of the pommel horse. You can practice techniques for the pommel horse on other pieces of equipment before trying the pommel horse.

WALKING ON PARALLEL BARS

You can build up your upper body strength for the pommel horse by doing walks along the parallel bars.

By practicing walking up and down the parallel bars, you will get used to holding your weight. Remember to chalk up, so that you do not slip on the bars. Mount the bars from a platform. Push down through your shoulders and be aware not to shrug your shoulders. By pressing down with straight arms, you will be able to hold your bodyweight up and keep a straight body position. Keep your legs straight and toes pointed.

To start walking, you will need to create movement in your body. Lift one hand up and move it along the bar, this allows your weight to transfer and the movement to happen.

Then center yourself and lift the other hand and place it further along the bar. This exercise will help to build up your upper body strength.

 TOP TIP
Do a lot of upper body conditioning, as the more strength you build up in this area, the easier it will be to develop your skills on the pommel horse.

To master front support swings on the pommel horse, you must do a series of progressions. Included here are two for the parallel bars and the rings. When you build up your strength and master the technique, you can then perform them on the pommel horse with greater ease.

Place your lower arms on the parallel bars or through the rings to support your weight and swing your legs side to side in a straddle position.
Keep your legs straight and extend at the end of the swing.

Use your lower arms to support your weight on the parallel bars.

Legs straight and in straddle position

Your legs should be straight and extended at the end of each swing.

Young gymnasts will start learning skills for the pommel horse on the mushroom.
This is a small, rounded piece of equipment which allows gymnasts to perform circle movements easier and for a lot longer than performing on the handles of the pommel horse.

FRONT SUPPORT SWINGS

Having practiced the progressions on the parallel bars and on the rings, you should move on to trying them on the pommel horse. When doing front support swings, the legs should remain straddled throughout without closing the straddle at the bottom of the swing. Extend the straddle at the end of your swing.

STEP 1

Hold yourself in the front support position on the pommel horse.

Lean slightly away from the horse.

Swing your leg upward in a vertical position.

STEP 2

In the swing your bodyweight should transfer from your upper leg to your support arm.

Support arm

Your other arm can lift off from the handle.

Straight leg

Support arm

Straight leg

Start to drive lower leg upward.

STEP 3

The height and form should be equal at both sides of the swing. Your legs should be straight and you should try to achieve height at the end of the swing.

STEP 4

As your top leg reaches its peak, you should think about driving the bottom leg upward. Don't wait until your other leg has come down.

The front shears are a progression from the front support swings. It is a difficult move as you have to switch your legs over to bring one in front of the horse.

Take weight on your support arm.

STEP 1

Start with a front support swing. Your legs should be in straddle position with your right leg high and your left leg at the bottom of the swing.

STEP 2

Before you replace your right hand on the pommel, swing your right leg down in front of the horse. At the same time drive your left leg up as you would with a front support swing.

Transfer weight so that your other arm becomes the support arm.

Lift your arm and swing your leg down behind the horse.

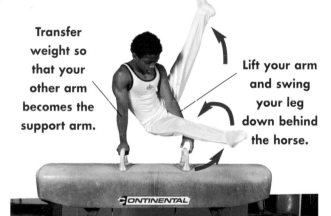

STEP 3

When your left leg reaches the top of the swing transfer your weight onto your right arm and lift your left arm off the pommel. As you lift your left arm swing your right leg under it.

STEP 4

This is where you switch legs. As your right leg swings under your arm and back behind the horse, drive your left leg down in front of the horse. Replace your left arm on the pommel and get ready to repeat the move on the other side.

TOP TIP
Work on your flexibility. With increased hip flexibility you can achieve more elevation at the top of each swing.

THE BEAM

The beam requires poise and balance. A routine is composed of a mount, acrobatic elements, leaps, turns, dance, and a dismount. You should perform with confidence and maintain a good center of balance so that you don't fall off the apparatus. The top gymnasts on this apparatus perform with as much ease on the beam as if they were performing the routine on the floor.

FRONT SUPPORT MOUNT

There are various mounts you can perform to get onto the beam.

This gymnast is demonstrating the front support mount. You can jump up to this position by using a springboard. Your head should look up when you reach this front support position. To stand up on the beam, lift one leg over and sit in a straddle. Then put your legs behind you and push up on your toes.

You should keep your arms and legs straight and toes pointed.

STAG MOUNT

This is the stag mount, where the gymnast runs up to the beam, bounces onto the springboard and leaps onto the beam, with the leading leg bent at the knee and the back leg straight and extended.

In the stag leap, the front leg is bent and then opened for landing.

WALKING ALONG THE BEAM

It takes time to build up your confidence on the beam. Practice by doing different walks as part of your beam warm-up session. *Keeping a tight body and looking straight forward will help to maintain your balance.*

Walk along the beam lifting one leg up high, with your toes pointed.

Walk along the beam on your toes with your arms up by your ears.

A good forward roll should be a fluid and smooth movement.
Practice the forward roll on the floor, then move to the low beam and gain confidence before doing the move on the high beam. Use a beam mat which will give you some support for your back. Remove the mat when both you and your coach feel confident that you can perform it on the high beam.

STEP 1
Crouch down.

STEP 2
Place the heels of your hands on the beam.

Tuck your head in.

Push off with your feet.

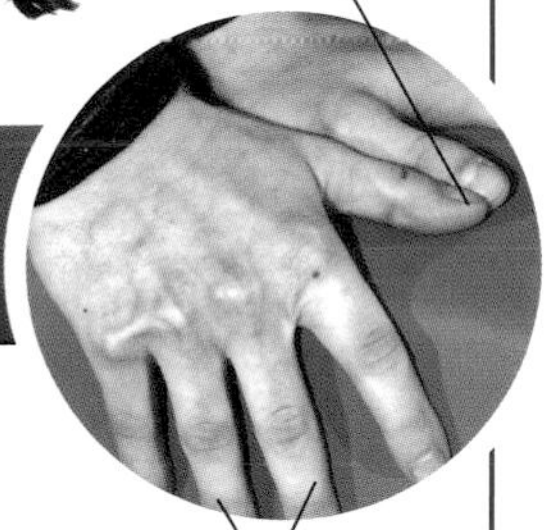

Thumbs should point forward.

STEP 3
Roll over. Your spine should be along the center of the beam.

STEP 4
Continue the roll and put your weight on the landing foot to finish and reach out in front of you.

Fingers should be pointing down the sides of the beam.

TOP TIP
Draw a straight line on a mat with chalk to practice your gymnastics moves before moving to the low beam, and then to the high beam.

BACK WALKOVER

There are many moves in gymnastics that involve being upside down. These moves require you to put all your weight on to your hands. This gymnast is performing a back walkover.
When you pass through the handstand your legs should be split and straight. Your hands are flat and you will be aware of where to put your standing leg down, so that you do not lose your balance. This movement is also commonly performed going the opposite way, which is called a front walkover.

FREE FORWARD ROLL

The free forward roll is a more advanced skill, it involves doing a forward roll without using your hands.
To start with you should practice with a beam mat. Imagine you are rolling your spine along a straight line. Bend your landing leg so it is ready to plant firmly on the beam when you come out of the roll. Then you can stand up.

Hand position is very important. You should always have your hands flat on the beam to avoid injuries.

Your arms should be straight and not touching the beam.

Beam mat

This is a soft mat which is placed over the beam to give you added support when practicing new moves.

To leave the beam and to jump up into the air, requires confidence and practice.
At first, you can practice doing low jumps. It is important to practice your landing on the beam. Smaller gymnasts are able to stand on the beam and perform movements, landing with their two ankles beside each other. However, most gymnasts land with one foot slightly in front of the other.

Bring your arms behind you, then swing them forward and upward so that they are beside your ears.

TUCK JUMP

To do a tuck jump on the beam, bend your knees and bring your arms behind you.
Then swing your arms forward and upward (this will achieve height in the jump), and push off from the beam with your feet and knees.

Bend your knees as you jump and bring both knees up toward your chest.

SPLIT LEAP

If you are very flexible you will be able to achieve a good leg extension in your split leap.
Practicing your splits while sitting on the floor will increase the range of movement in your hips. Increase your confidence at performing this movement by practicing it on the low beam, then move up to the high beam. To achieve height in your leap, push off hard from your leading leg.

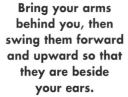

TOP TIP
Your arms help keep your body in line with the beam. Keep your arms tight and straight as you perform moves. This will help you to balance.

HIGH BAR

Perhaps the most breathtaking piece of apparatus in men's gymnastics is the high bar. Elite gymnasts perform "giants," which are rotational moves around the bar in the handstand position. This allows the gymnast to build up speed and wind up into big release moves and dismounts with multiple somersaults and twists.

THE CAST

The cast is a move where you swing your legs back and away from the bar up to a horizontal position. Maintaining body tension is essential in order to perform a good cast.

The cast on the bar is also known as a "beat." Think of yourself as beating away from the bar. A common error is for gymnasts to separate their legs at the end of the beat or cast backward, as they try and achieve more height. Try to imagine that your legs are glued together at all times so that they don't come apart.

STEP 1
Start in front support. Move your shoulders in front of the bar.

Keep your body tight and in a hollow position.

Drive your legs backward.

STEP 2
Swing your legs forward to get momentum.

STEP 3

Keep your arms straight and your shoulders forward until your hips are above shoulder height.

Beat your legs backward.

Arms straight

STEP 4

Press forward with your hands on the bar as you raise your legs to open the angle between your body and your shoulders.

Control your swing back down to front support.

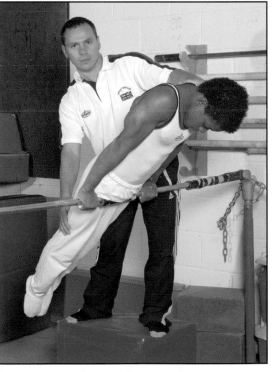

Once you have mastered a good cast to front support, the next progression is for your coach to help you perform a cast up to a handstand on the low bar.

 **TOP TIP**

Tie a pair of socks around your shins so that you can get used to casting backward with your legs held together.

THE BACKWARD HIP CIRCLE

*T*he backward hip circle is usually performed after the cast. Not only is this move performed on the high bar and asymmetric bars, but it can also be performed on the beam by jumping up to front support and then rotating around the beam.

BACKWARD HIP CIRCLE

This movement involves your whole body circling backward around the bar.
The move begins when the shoulders begin to lean backward, which causes the rest of the body to follow. You must keep your hips close to the bar so you rotate the whole way around it. Performing this move after a cast gives you momentum so that you can go straight into the backward hip circle, and you will rotate around the bar.

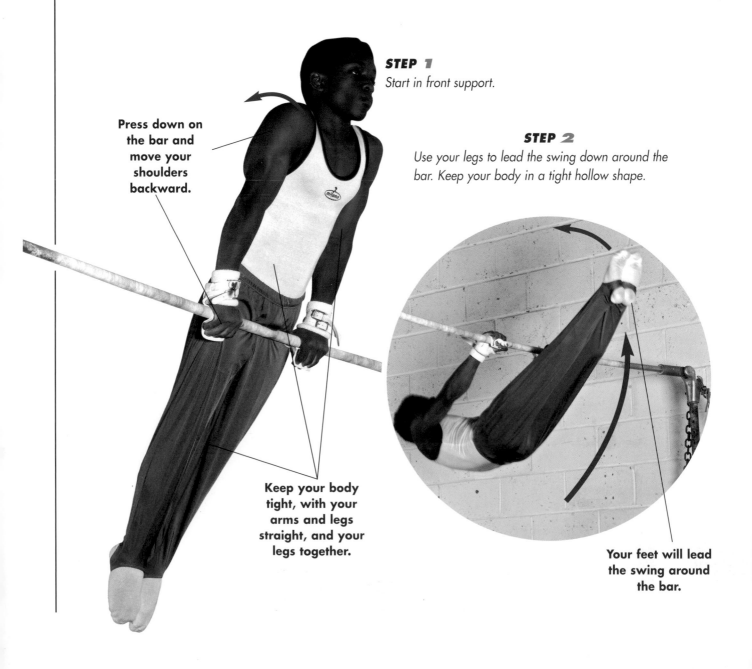

Press down on the bar and move your shoulders backward.

STEP 1
Start in front support.

STEP 2
Use your legs to lead the swing down around the bar. Keep your body in a tight hollow shape.

Keep your body tight, with your arms and legs straight, and your legs together.

Your feet will lead the swing around the bar.

Rotate wrists

Regrasp bar

Press bar on to thighs

STEP 3
You must stay close to the bar in the rotation by pressing the bar on to your thighs.

STEP 4
Continue rotating around the bar and finish in the front support position by pushing up onto your straight arms.

TOP TIP
Remember to chalk up and wear grips so that you have better control on the bar.

COMPETITION

The biggest event on the gymnastics calendar is the Olympic Games, which is held every four years.
The World Championships are the qualifying event for the Olympic Games. Countries from around the world send their top gymnasts to compete as a team at the World Championships. The countries with the top teams can send gymnasts to the Olympic Games. All gymnasts compete in a qualification round, through which they can qualify for the team final, the **all-around** *final, and the individual apparatus final. Other major competitions on the gymnastics calendar include the U.S. National Championships, European Championships, and the Commonwealth Games.*

Daiane dos Santos of Brazil performs on the floor in the World Championships.

NATIONAL SQUADS

To compete at international level requires years of training and competing. Gymnasts work their way up by competing at regional level.
A select few are then chosen for the junior national squad before moving up to the senior squad when they are old enough. At national squad level, gymnasts will perform in many competitions so that they get used to competing in front of an audience and learn how to cope with nerves and pressure.

FIG

The governing body for gymnastics is the Federation Internationale de Gymnastique (FIG).
The FIG produces the rulebook of gymnastics known as the **"Code of Points."** *This document is updated and revised at the end of every Olympic cycle. It sets out the difficulty value of each skill and what the requirements are for each piece of apparatus.*

In 1997, the FIG introduced an age limit for international competitions.

The minimum age to compete is 16 years old. Having an age limit means that younger gymnasts do not compete at a level that is too high and experience too much stress. It also gives older gymnasts the chance to keep competing.

The most significant change in the "Code of Points" has been the abolition of the perfect "10."

Gymnastics now uses open-ended scoring. There are two panels of judges, one panel judges the difficulty of the routine, the other panel judges the execution (how well it is performed).

Judges view a performance of a gymnast on the pommel horse.

A value = 0.1 points	
B value = 0.2 points	
C value = 0.3 points	
D value = 0.4 points	
E value = 0.5 points	
F value = 0.6 points	
G value = 0.7 points	

There are specific elements that a gymnast must perform in their routine and these requirements will vary depending on the level of competition.

Elements are graded from A to G, with A being the easiest and G the hardest.

DIET

A gymnast needs fuel to be able to train and a balanced diet will ensure he or she is getting all the necessary vitamins and minerals. A balanced diet should combine carbohydrates, fat, protein, and fiber.

This diagram shows the percentage of different foods that should be eaten to maintain a balanced diet.

Drink liquids little and often. Avoid sugary drinks as they provide no nutrient value, are loaded with calories and are gas-forming.

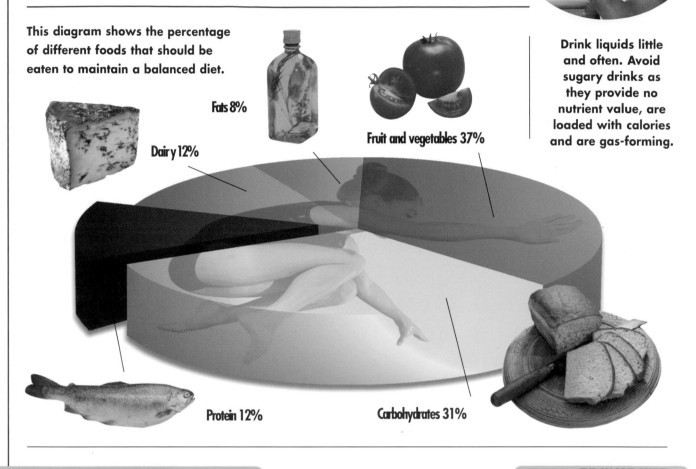

Fats 8%

Dairy 12%

Fruit and vegetables 37%

Protein 12%

Carbohydrates 31%

CARBOHYDRATES, FATS, AND PROTEINS

Carbohydrates, fats, and proteins are the nutrients which provide energy.

Foods like pasta, rice, potatoes, bread, and cereal contain carbohydrates. They release the energy required for dynamic training and explosive energy immediately. Fats and proteins supply energy over a longer period of training. Protein is found in animal products, such as meat, poultry, fish, and dairy foods. Having fresh fruits and vegetables in your daily diet will provide you with vitamins and minerals.

THE CALORIE COUNT

Elite gymnasts keep a watchful eye on their calorie intake in order to control their weight.

All food that we eat contains a number of calories. Foods which are high in fat contain more calories and require more exercise to burn off. Active gymnasts will burn around 3,000 to 3,500 calories per day, so they must eat this amount of calories in order for their weight to remain the same.

 TOP TIP
Eat about one and a half hours before a training session. This gives enough time for the food to be properly digested. Eating a snack one and a half hours after training is also a good idea.

MENTAL ATTITUDE

Getting to the top in gymnastics requires long hours of training and also a strong mental focus. It requires a lot of time away from friends and family, as gymnasts must travel to competitions and training camps. Rest is also very important, as it allows both body and mind to recover after a work-out.

THE COACH

A gymnastics coach should always encourage a gymnast and take the athlete through the correct progressions in order for the gymnast to advance in a manner that is appropriate. *The safety and welfare of gymnasts should always be of the highest importance. Goal-setting will motivate gymnasts to train to develop skills and work toward performing them in competition. Sometimes, a gymnast experiences disappointment. This can be difficult to deal with and requires positive thinking, and a lot of support from his or her coach. After competing, the coach and gymnast sit down and talk about the competition, set out goals for the next competition, and adapt the training program if necessary.*

Gymnast and coach in discussion—getting in to the zone.

CONCENTRATION

A high level of concentration is required in training and when competing. *It is important to perform safely and stay focused as this will minimize the risk of injury. **Psychologists** help gymnasts to focus their mind using different strategies. Thinking positive thoughts, such as "I can do this," creates a positive mental attitude. Gymnasts are also trained to visualize what they want to achieve. Whether it's mastering a certain skill or winning the gold medal in a competition, a positive focus is a powerful influence.*

Gymnasts need good concentration to perform at the highest level.

HOW THE FAMOUS DO IT

Although gymnastics has been around for more than 2,000 years, it has been a competitive sport for little more than 100 years. During this time, the sport of gymnastics has changed a lot and routines have become more and more spectacular.

DEVELOPING ELEMENTS

Up until the 1960s, gymnastics remained mostly a male sport, dominated by gymnasts who were known for their strength.

The top nations at the time were Japan and the Soviet Union. The difficulty of skills being performed was always being increased, new skills were being introduced, and gymnasts who were the first to perform them had those skills named after them. Alexander Tkatchev performed a high level release move on the bar in 1976, and the Tkatchev is still being performed today.

WOMEN SUPERSTARS

Olga Korbut (Belarus)

Traditionally, women gymnasts performed with grace and their movements were slow and controlled, a style which was made famous by Soviet gymnast Ludmilla Tourischeva, who won the all-around gold at the 1972 Olympic Games.

In the 1970s some truly remarkable gymnasts caused a sensation that would change women's gymnastics forever. With her tiny body and big personality, Soviet gymnast Olga Korbut won the hearts of millions at the 1972 Olympic Games in Munich. Korbut helped turn women's gymnastics into the popular sport it is now and inspired a whole new generation of children to do gymnastics. Standing only 4.8 feet (1.49 m) tall, the 17 year old performed incredibly difficult routines. Her back salto on the beam was regarded as a daring move and her floor exercise sparkled. She became known as the "Munchkin of Munich," the darling of the Olympics.

Also credited for popularizing the sport, is Nadia Comaneci, a 14-year-old Romanian who, under the guidance of her coach Bela Karolyi, set a new standard in gymnastics—that of perfection.

Her performance on the asymmetric bars at the 1976 Montreal Olympics earned her the first-ever perfect "10" in the history of the sport. She went on to score six more perfect scores and win three gold medals at these Olympics.

CURRENT OLYMPIC ALL-AROUND CHAMPIONS (BEIJING, 2008)

The powerhouse nations such as the U.S.A., Russia, and China continue to produce superstars in the sport. Their daredevil performances and high-level skills amaze audiences around the world.

Nastia Liukin (U.S.A.)

Anastasia Liukin, or Nastia as she is known, won the Olympic all-around final at the 2008 Olympic Games in Beijing. Liukin is the only child of two former Soviet champions, Valeri Liukin and Anna Kotchneva. The family moved to America when Nastia was two years old and now live in Texas. Nastia is admired in the gymnastics world for her grace and elegant long lines.

Yang Wei (CHINA)

Chinese gymnast Yang Wei is best known for his impressive ability on all six pieces of apparatus. He won the all-around title at the 2008 Olympic Games in Beijing.

WHAT HAPPENS NEXT?

After a career competing in gymnastics, many gymnasts often go into coaching, or study to become a judge.

Some gymnasts earn scholarships with colleges where they can continue to train while furthering their education. Other gymnasts who have achieved world success turn professional, which means they are paid for all their commercial appearances.

GLOSSARY

abdominals *Also known as "abs," these are the stomach muscles*

all-around *Competition format in which the gymnast competes on every piece of apparatus*

apparatus *The equipment male and female gymnasts perform and compete on*

arch *When the body is in arch position the back is curved back and the arms and legs are stretched backward*

ballet bar *A bar made of metal or wood, which gymnasts hold on to and practice ballet moves on*

blocking *Keeping your arms fully extended and straight and pushing through your shoulders*

choreographer *A professional who creates dance routines*

code of points *The rule book of gymnastics*

conditioning *A physical preparation program to improve strength*

demi-plié *A ballet position which involves bending your knees while keeping your heels on the floor*

hamstrings *The muscles at the back of your thighs*

hollow *When the body is in hollow position the back is curved forward and the arms and legs are forward*

pike *A position where the body is bent at the hips and legs are straight and raised toward the trunk of the body, forming a "L" shape*

poise *Performing a movement with grace and elegance*

psychologist *An expert in dealing with the way the mind works*

splits *A position where the legs are extended in opposite directions either one in front of you and one behind, or out to the sides*

straddle *A position where the legs are open wide and extended in front of the body*

tuck *A position where the legs are bent and raised toward the trunk of the body*

warm up *Exercises performed at the beginning of a training session to get the body and muscles warm*

INDEX

Printed in the U.S.A. — CG